Fun Fan Facts:
The Unofficial NBA Edition

Houston Rockets

Everything Young Houston Rockets
Fans Should Know

By: Jake Liam

Dedication

For the Red Nation. You cheer louder than a rocket launch. And that is saying something.

THE NBA
BY THE NUMBERS

MOST NBA CHAMPIONSHIPS*

CELTICS (18) †

LAKERS (17)

WARRIORS (7)

BULLS (6)

SPURS (5)

As of the 2024-25 Season. † One Trophy = 4 Championships.

NBA HISTORY SNAPSHOT

1946 — NBA Founded

1954 — Shot Clock Introduced

1979 — 3-Point Line Added

2023 — NBA Cup Introduced

BIG NUMBERS

$156 million
Stephen Curry's est. earnings in the 24-25 season

7'7"
Tallest player in NBA history (Gheorghe Mureşan & Manute Bol)

30
Teams Competing in the NBA

4
Playoff Rounds

82
Games Per Season

HOUSTON ROCKETS
IN THE NBA

- FOUNDED: 1967 †
- NBA TITLES: 2
- CONFERENCE TITLES: 4*

22
Game Wining Streak - Longest in NBA History

*† Founding dates are complicated & may cause arguments at Thanksgiving. Ask someone born before color TV. All Titles reflect pre-relocation franchise history. * As of 2024-25 Season.*

NBA ALL-TIME MVP LEADERS

KAREEM ABDUL-JABBAR (6) ★ MICHAEL JORDAN (5) ★ BILL RUSSELL (5)

EASTERN CONFERENCE

Atlantic – **Celtics**
Atlantic – **Nets**
Atlantic – **Knicks**
Atlantic – **76ers**
Atlantic – **Raptors**
Central – **Bulls**
Central – **Cavaliers**
Central – **Pistons**
Central – **Pacers**
Central – **Bucks**
Southeast – **Hawks**
Southeast – **Hornets**
Southeast – **Heat**
Southeast – **Magic**
Southeast – **Wizards**

WESTERN CONFERENCE

Pacific – **Lakers**
Pacific – **Clippers**
Pacific – **Warriors**
Pacific – **Suns**
Pacific – **Kings**
Northwest – **Nuggets**
Northwest – **Timberwolves**
Northwest – **Thunder**
Northwest – **Trail Blazers**
Northwest – **Jazz**
Southwest – **Mavericks**
Southwest – **Rockets**
Southwest – **Spurs**
Southwest – **Pelicans**
Southwest – **Grizzlies**

Introduction

Welcome, fans! Whether you're new to cheering for the Houston Rockets or you've been bleeding the team colors your whole life, this book is packed with fun, exciting facts about your favorite team. Get ready to impress your friends and family with everything you know about the Houston Rockets.

Quick Time Out

This book is packed with stats. Like, A LOT of stats. Every fact was checked, double-checked, and triple-checked. But here's the thing about basketball history: not everyone agrees on everything. Ask someone who watched games before color TV and someone who grew up with instant replay and you'll get two completely different answers. My dad, stepdad, uncle, and grandpa all argued about the same fact. Four people. Four answers. All of them think they're right. So if you spot something that doesn't match what you've heard, congratulations. You might be a bigger fan than the people who helped make this book. And honestly? That's pretty cool.

HOW IT WORKS

THE SEASON

82 Games. One Goal.

Each team plays 82 games.
Win enough to make the
Playoffs.
Every game counts!

PLAYOFFS

30 Teams. 16 Make It.

8 per conference make the playoffs.
Win=Advance | Lose=Go Home
Best record
gets home court!

PLAYOFF ROUNDS

Best of 7. Win 4 or Go Home.

4 rounds of pure pressure.
Every series is do-or-die!

OVERTIME?

5 More Minutes.

Keep playing until
someone pulls ahead.
No ties. Ever.

THE FINALS

One Series. One Champion.

Winner lifts the Trophy.
Legend status unlocked.

How the NBA Works

At first glance, basketball feels simple. Ten players. One ball. Two hoops. Go.

Then the NBA adds the layers.

An 82-game regular season. A draft where bad teams pick first. Playoffs that last two full months. Superstars who can change everything with one trade. Dynasties that rise, fall, and rise again.

And somehow, it all works.

The NBA is built on one big idea: every team gets a chance to reset, reload, and rise again. No relegation. No dropping down to a lower league. Just basketball, every night, from October through June.

It is a league designed for drama, stars, and comebacks. And once you understand the flow, it is impossible to stop watching.

The League Setup

The NBA has 30 teams, spread across the United States and Canada. Those teams are split into two conferences:

- Eastern Conference
- Western Conference

Each conference has three divisions, mostly based on geography. Divisions matter for scheduling, but not as much as they used to.

Every team plays 82 regular season games, usually from October through April. Home games. Road games. Back-to-back nights. Long road trips. The season is a marathon before the sprint even starts.

Win games, and you climb the standings. Lose too many, and the pressure builds fast.

How Games Are Played

An NBA game has four quarters, each lasting 12 minutes. That means 48 minutes of game time, plus timeouts, free throws, and the occasional coach argument that adds another 20 minutes nobody planned for.

Scoring is simple:

- A shot inside the three-point line is worth 2 points
- A shot beyond the arc is worth 3 points
- Free throws are worth 1 point

If the score is tied at the end of regulation, the game goes to overtime, which lasts 5 minutes. Still tied? Another overtime. Keep going until someone wins.

There is a shot clock too. Teams have 24 seconds to take a shot. No standing around. No holding the ball forever. Keep it moving.

The Regular Season Race

The regular season is long for a reason. It tests everything.

Depth. Health. Focus. Patience.

Teams play opponents from both conferences, but they face conference rivals more often. By the end of the season, each conference's top teams have earned their playoff spots the hard way.

The goal is simple: make the playoffs. But there is a twist.

The NBA Cup

In 2023, the NBA added something new to the middle of the season. Something with actual stakes. They called it the In-Season Tournament, now known as the NBA Cup.

It works like this: Every team plays a small group stage during November and December, with special court designs that look like nothing else in basketball. The best teams advance to a knockout round held in Las Vegas.

The winners split a prize pool. Players earn bonus money. And for the first time, a team could lift a trophy before the playoffs even started.

Some fans are still warming up to it. Some players love it. But the moment a team starts treating it seriously and a crowd shows up buzzing in December, it feels like something.

Which, honestly, sounds about right.

The Play-In Tournament

Instead of sending the top eight teams from each conference straight to the playoffs, the NBA added something new. The Play-In Tournament.

Here is how it works:

- Teams ranked 1 through 6 in each conference are safe
- Teams ranked 7 through 10 fight for the final two playoff spots

The 7 and 8 seeds have an advantage. Win once and you are in. Lose and you still get one more shot. The 9 and 10 seeds have to win twice in a row just to earn a first-round matchup.

It turns the end of the season into a sprint. Every game suddenly matters more. Fans love it. Coaches age rapidly.

The NBA Playoffs

Once the playoffs begin, everything tightens.

Sixteen teams enter. Eight from each conference. Every round is a best-of-seven games series. That means the first team to win four games moves on:

- First Round
- Conference Semifinals
- Conference Finals
- NBA Finals

Home-court advantage matters. Crowds get louder. Rotations get shorter. Superstars play heavier minutes. One bad quarter can flip a series. One great performance can define a career.

By the time the NBA Finals arrive in June, only two teams are left. One from the East. One from the West.

Four wins away from a championship. Four wins away from history.

The NBA Draft: Hope Begins Here

Here is where the NBA gets clever. Every summer, new players enter the league through the NBA Draft. Teams take turns selecting college players, international stars, and teenagers straight out of high school.

The teams that finished with the worst records get the best odds to pick early through the Draft Lottery. It is not guaranteed, but it gives struggling franchises a real shot at changing their future with one pick.

That means one bad season does not doom you forever. It might actually change everything. Some franchises are rebuilt by a single draft night moment.

Hope shows up wearing a new jersey.

No Relegation. All Pressure.

Unlike many global sports leagues, NBA teams never drop down to a lower league. They always stay in the NBA.

That does not mean there is no pressure.

Fans remember losing seasons. Owners make changes. Coaches get replaced. Players get traded. Every year is a test of direction, patience, and belief.

Stars, Systems, and Showtime

The NBA is famous for its stars. But stars do not win alone.

Teams need chemistry. Coaches need systems. Role players need to deliver on the biggest stages. One injury. One hot streak. One trade deadline deal. Any of it can flip a season.

That balance between individual brilliance and team basketball is what makes the league special.

Fast breaks. Buzzer-beaters. Game 7s. And moments that get replayed forever. That is the NBA.

Once you get the flow, it is pure electricity.

Houston Rockets Facts

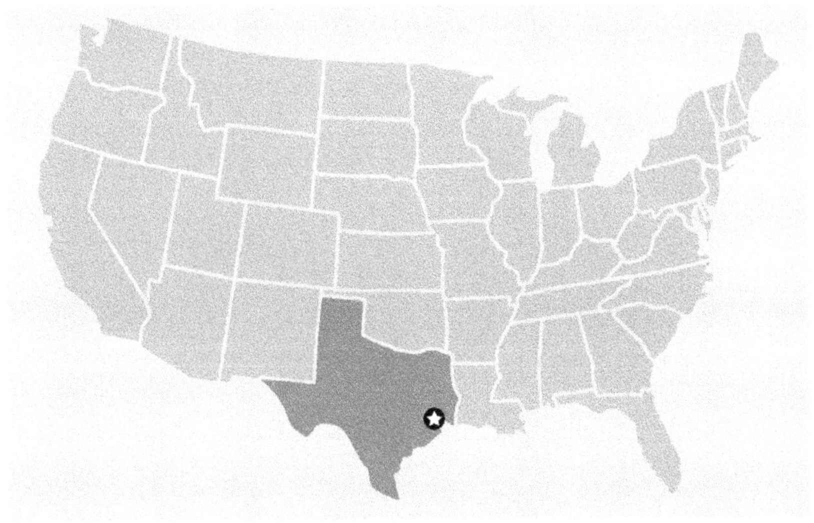

Home City

Houston, Texas

Home City Metro Area Population

about 7.5 million

Home Arena

Toyota Center

Max Capacity: 18,055

Famous Local Food

BBQ, Tex-Mex, Gulf shrimp, kolaches, Vietnamese food

Conference / Division

Western / Southwest

Chapter 1: Rockets Ignition: How Houston Got Its Team

1. From San Diego to Houston: A Franchise Finds Its City

The Houston Rockets did not start in Houston. Take a second with that. The team that would one day win two NBA championships, produce one of the greatest players who ever lived, and make an entire city lose its mind over basketball started its life in San Diego, California, in 1967. San Diego. Beaches. Sunshine. Tacos. Lovely place. Zero rocket energy.

The name made a little bit of sense at the time. San Diego had a growing aerospace industry, so calling a basketball team the Rockets was meant to feel futuristic and cool. What was not cool was the attendance. Fans were not exactly breaking down doors to watch a losing team in a half-empty arena. After four rough seasons, ownership looked at the situation, looked at Houston, and made a decision. Houston was booming. Houston had a new arena. Houston wanted a team badly. So the Rockets packed their bags and headed to Texas in 1971.

Here is the part that makes the whole story almost too perfect. Houston is home to NASA's Johnson Space Center. The actual command center for American space missions. The place where the moon landing was directed from. Someone named a basketball team the Rockets and accidentally moved them to the one city on Earth where the name was completely, perfectly, obviously correct. Nobody planned it. It just landed. Pun absolutely intended.

2. Space City: The Name That Was Always Meant for Houston

Houston has a thing with space. Not in a 'we have a cool museum' kind of way. In a 'we literally helped put humans on the moon' kind of way. NASA chose Houston as home to its Mission Control Center in 1961, and from that moment on, the city had an identity unlike anywhere else in America. This is where astronauts train. This is where every major space mission gets talked through, sweated over, and celebrated. This is where someone once said 'Houston, we have a problem' and the whole world knew exactly where to call.

Now drop a team called the Rockets into that city and tell me it does not fit like a perfect layup. The red and gold colors. The rocket on the court. The launch-sequence energy every time the crowd gets going. Other cities have cute nicknames. Houston has an actual space program. When a Rockets player takes off for a dunk, he is doing it in the same city where humans figured out how to leave the planet entirely. That is a seriously good backdrop for a basketball game.

Imagine this: you are sitting in Toyota Center, the Rockets are on a ten-point run, the arena is shaking, and somewhere a few miles away there are engineers tracking satellites. That is just a Tuesday in Houston.

3. Moses Malone: The Big Man Who Started It All (1976-1982)

Moses Malone skipped college and went straight to the pros out of high school in 1974, making him one of the very first players ever to do it. The league he joined, the ABA, did not survive long enough to make a big deal out of it. Moses survived just fine. When the ABA folded in 1976, Houston grabbed him, and the Rockets immediately became a team worth watching.

What Moses did was rebound. Not just well. Historically, almost-rudely, somebody-please-stop-him levels of rebounding. He led the NBA in boards six different times. He once averaged more than 17 rebounds per game for a full season. To understand how ridiculous that is, a really excellent rebounder today might pull down 12 or 13 per game. Moses did nearly double that, regularly, and still had energy left over to score 20 points a night. He treated missed shots the way a golden retriever treats a tennis ball. Every single one was his.

He eventually left for Philadelphia, where he won a championship in 1983 and delivered one of the most confident playoff predictions in sports history. But that's a different book. Houston fans will never forget what he built here. Moses arrived when this franchise needed a foundation. He gave them one, plus about 17 rebounds on top of it.

4. The 1981 Finals Run: Nobody Told Houston It Was Not Supposed to Happen

The Houston Rockets finished the 1980-81 regular season with 40 wins. Not bad. Not exactly terrifying either. Teams with 40 wins do not usually end up two wins from a championship. Houston had other ideas.

They knocked off the Los Angeles Lakers in the first round. The Lakers had Magic Johnson and Kareem Abdul-Jabbar and basically the entire basketball world on their side. Houston beat them in three games. Then they beat the San Antonio Spurs to reach the NBA Finals, where they faced the Boston Celtics, one of the most decorated teams in the history of the sport. Larry Bird. Robert Parish. Kevin McHale. The whole terrifying collection. The Rockets pushed them to six games before the road finally ran out.

A 40-win team came within two wins of the whole thing. Moses Malone was the engine, grabbing every loose ball in sight and giving Houston extra possessions that no other team could manufacture. The city that had only recently gotten this franchise suddenly could not stop talking about it. Houston did not win the title that year. But something changed. The Rockets stopped being a team people ignored and started being a team people feared. That is not nothing. That is actually everything.

5. Rudy T: The Coach Who Refused to Quit (1991-2003)

Before Rudy Tomjanovich ever coached a game, he was already one of the most remarkable stories in the league. In 1977, during a fight on the court, he was hit so hard that doctors were genuinely concerned about whether he would live. The injuries were severe enough that most people assumed his career was over before they even worried about whether he would walk out of the hospital.

He walked out. He came back and played four more seasons. That comeback alone would have been enough story for most people. Rudy was not most people. He joined the Rockets' coaching staff, worked his way up quietly, became head coach in 1991, and then did something that sounds like it was made up: he won back-to-back NBA championships in 1994 and 1995. Two titles. Consecutive years. In a league where winning one is almost impossibly hard.

He stood at the podium after winning the 1995 title and told the world: Don't ever underestimate the heart of a champion. Eight words. Still echoing. A man who had been knocked down as hard as any athlete ever has been, came all the way back to coach two championship teams. If you tried to write that as a movie script, someone would tell you it was too much. Rudy T did not ask for anyone's permission. He just kept showing up and winning until nobody could argue with the results.

6. Hakeem "The Dream" Olajuwon: The Greatest Rocket Ever (1984-2001)

Hakeem Olajuwon grew up in Lagos, Nigeria, playing handball and soccer. He did not pick up a basketball until he was seventeen years old. Seventeen. Most NBA players have been dribbling since they could walk. Hakeem started late, learned fast, and somehow became the greatest center of his generation anyway. The nerve of this guy.

Houston drafted him first overall in 1984, and from day one it was obvious that something special was happening. Hakeem had footwork so smooth that coaches invented a name for it: the Dream Shake. What nobody knew watching him spin and fake in the post was that the footwork traced directly back to Lagos, where Hakeem had played soccer as a goalkeeper, using his size and quick feet to stop shots at the other end of a completely different game.

He would catch the ball in the post, fake left, fake right, spin, pump fake, and by the time the defender figured out what was happening, the ball was already going through the net. He won back-to-back NBA championships in 1994 and 1995, was named Finals MVP both times, and is still the only player in NBA history to win Finals MVP, regular season MVP, and Defensive Player of the Year all in the same season. He blocked shots. He scored. He played defense like it was personal. And he did it all starting from a country where almost nobody played basketball.

Two future legends. One finger up. Message received. Michael Jordan and Hakeem Olajuwon pose with the 'number one' sign after being picked at the top of the famous 1984 NBA Draft. One went to the Chicago Bulls, the other to the Houston Rockets. Two Hall of Famers. A lot of championships. And one very crowded GOAT conversation. *Photo: Michael Jordan and Hakeem Olajuwon. Photograph via Wikimedia Commons. Public domain. Source: Wikimedia Commons.*

7. Clyde Drexler: The Trade That Put Houston Over the Top (1995)

Clyde Drexler grew up in Houston. He went to college in Houston at the University of Houston. He was basically Houston in a jersey. And yet when he became an NBA star, it was in Portland, Oregon, about 2,100 miles away. Life is funny sometimes.

Drexler spent twelve seasons as a Portland Trail Blazer, became one of the best shooting guards in the league, made the Finals in 1992, and was universally considered a future Hall of Famer. Then, in February 1995, with the Rockets already pretty good and gunning for a second straight title, Houston made the trade. Clyde came home. The city lost its mind in a completely reasonable way. Imagine your favorite player growing up down the street from you and one day they just show up on your team. That is what happened.

The pairing of Clyde and Hakeem was unstoppable. Two superstars. Two Houston legends. One shared goal. The Rockets went on to win the 1995 championship, and Drexler finally got the ring that had slipped away in Portland three years earlier. He celebrated in the city where he grew up, with one of his oldest friends on the planet. Some things in sports are so perfectly arranged that you spend ten minutes afterwards just staring at the ceiling thinking about them. This was one of those things.

8. Charles Barkley: The Round Mound Comes to Space City (1996-2000)

Charles Barkley is one of the most entertaining humans to ever play professional basketball. He was loud. He was funny. He was brutally honest. He once said on live television that he was not a role model, which caused a national debate that lasted years. He also averaged 22 points and 11 rebounds per game for his career while listed at 6 feet 6 inches but widely suspected to be shorter, lighter, and somehow more powerful than anyone his size had any business being.

Houston traded for Barkley in 1996 to pair him with Hakeem and Drexler, which on paper was the most terrifying trio of thirty-somethings the Western Conference had ever seen. Fans called them the 'Three Kings.' They were old by basketball standards, collectively carrying enough mileage to make a mechanic nervous, and yet they were genuinely dangerous. They reached the Conference Finals in 1997 before losing to the Utah Jazz.

He never won a championship, which remains one of the great what-ifs in NBA history. But Barkley in Houston was never dull. He scored, he rebounded, he said things that ended up on the news, and he gave Rockets fans four years of must-watch basketball. Some players make a team better. Barkley made the whole situation more interesting. Both things matter.

9. Yao Ming: The 7-Foot-6 Giant Who Changed Everything (2002-2011)

Yao Ming was 7 feet 6 inches tall. That is not a typo. Seven. Six. The average NBA center stands around 6 feet 10 inches, which is already a height most humans never reach. Yao was eight inches taller than that. Standing next to a normal-sized person, he looked like a special effect.

He came to Houston from Shanghai, China, as the first overall pick in the 2002 draft, and scouts who had spent decades watching basketball had to recalibrate everything they thought they knew about what a center could look like. He was not just tall. He had footwork. He had touch. He had a mid-range jumper that floated in softly while defenders stood beneath him wondering what exactly they were supposed to do about this.

Opposing coaches would spend entire weeks preparing a game plan for Yao and then spend the actual game watching it fall apart in real time.

On the court he was genuinely dominant when healthy. He was a force in the post, a skilled passer, and surprisingly light on his feet for a man the size of a small building. Injuries cut his career shorter than anyone wanted, and he retired in 2011 at just 30 years old. What he did off the court, and what he meant to the sport globally, is a whole separate story that gets its own section later in this book, because it absolutely deserves one.

10. James Harden: The Beard, the Step-Back, and the Records (2012-2021)

James Harden has a beard so famous it has its own reputation. His beard arrived in Houston before the rest of him seemed to and somehow got even bigger over the years. We'll come back to that later.

Houston acquired him from Oklahoma City in 2012, and what followed was nine seasons of the most creative, statistically mind-bending scoring the league had seen in years. Harden led the NBA in scoring five times, four as a Rocket. He averaged 36.1 points per game in the

2018-19 season, the highest single-season average since Michael Jordan in 1987. His step-back three-pointer was a shot so difficult, so technically demanding, that other players spent entire summers trying to learn it and mostly just confused themselves. Harden did it in traffic. In crunch time. Against the best defenders alive. And he made it look relaxed, which was somehow the most annoying part.

He finished in the top three of MVP voting four years running and actually won the award in 2018. The championship never came, and how close the 2018 team got before falling apart is a story covered in Chapter 3 that will make your stomach hurt a little. But as a pure scorer, as a player who could get any shot he wanted from anywhere on the floor, James Harden was one of the most unstoppable offensive forces this franchise has ever seen. The beard just came with the package.

11. Clutch City Delivers Again: The 1995 Championship Run

The Houston Rockets were down three games to one against the Phoenix Suns in the 1995 playoffs. Three games to one. In a best-of-seven series, that is the basketball version of standing at the edge of a cliff. Most teams fall. Most fanbases start quietly making peace with the season ending. Houston did not get that memo.

The Rockets won three straight games to take the series. Then they went out and dismantled the top-seeded San Antonio Spurs in six games to reach the Finals. The Spurs had the best record in the NBA. It did not matter. A local newspaper had already given Houston its nickname the previous year, when the 1994 championship run inspired the headline 'Clutch City' for the first time. The 1995 playoffs did not invent the phrase. They just made it impossible to argue with.

They went on to win the 1995 championship, sweeping the Orlando Magic in the Finals in four games. Shaquille O'Neal was on that Magic team. A 23-year-old Shaq, enormous and terrifying and already one of the most dominant forces in basketball. Houston swept him. The Rockets beat a team with a 23-year-old Shaq and did not even need five games to do it. Clutch City was not a nickname. It was a statement.

12. Dream Shake: Hakeem Dismantles David Robinson and the Spurs (1995)

David Robinson was not a bad basketball player. Let us be very clear about that up front. He was a seven-foot Navy graduate, an Olympic gold medalist, a former Defensive Player of the Year, and one of the most physically impressive centers to ever put on an NBA uniform. He was excellent. He was legitimately great.

Hakeem Olajuwon just happened to be better. In the 1995 Western Conference Finals, Hakeem made David Robinson look like someone who had only recently learned what a basketball was. Game after game, Hakeem would catch the ball in the post, go into his Dream Shake routine, and Robinson would be left spinning in place while the ball went through the net. Spin. Fake. Pump fake. Reverse. Gone. Robinson knew what was coming and still could not stop it.

Hakeem averaged 35 points per game against Robinson across the series. Thirty-five. Against the reigning league MVP, who happened to also be one of the best defenders alive. It is widely considered one of the greatest individual playoff performances in NBA history. There is a 12-foot bronze statue of Hakeem standing outside Toyota Center right now, with his actual footprints set in cement nearby. Go find it. Stand in the footprints. Try to feel what it was like to guard him. You cannot. Nobody could.

13. The 1994 Championship: Houston's First Title, Against All Odds

The 1994 NBA Finals featured the Houston Rockets against the New York Knicks, and it went seven games, which is exactly what you want when two defensive-minded teams who genuinely dislike losing get together in June. This was not pretty basketball. It was grinding, bruising, every-possession-matters basketball. Kids today watch highlight reels from that series and the first thing they notice is how physical it was. The second thing they notice is that nobody was scared.

Game 7 was in Houston. The Summit was going absolutely wild. Hakeem was unstoppable, finishing with 25 points. The Rockets won 90-84 and the entire city exploded. It was Houston's first NBA championship, the payoff for everything, for Moses Malone's rebounds, for the 1981 Finals run that fell short, for every season the franchise had spent building toward something real.

Hakeem Olajuwon was named Finals MVP. Obviously. There was truly no other candidate. The man had carried this team on his back across an entire playoff run and made it look like he was out for a gentle evening jog. Houston had its championship. The city had waited long enough. Nobody cried. Well. Some people probably cried. You would have cried.

14. Yao vs. Shaq: The Rivalry the NBA Did Not Know It Needed

Shaquille O'Neal was, at his peak, the most physically dominant player in the NBA. He was 7 feet 1 inch tall and somewhere between 315 and 350 pounds depending on which scale you believed, and the scale probably did not matter much because Shaq was going to back you down regardless. Defenders bounced off him. Smaller centers just moved out of the way to preserve their health. It was completely reasonable behavior.

Then Yao Ming arrived. Seven feet six inches. Long arms. A post game he had been developing since his teenage years in China. And suddenly there was an actual matchup. Their first meeting on January 17, 2003, when the Los Angeles Lakers came to Houston, drew enormous television ratings in both the United States and China. Some say it was over 200 million viewers. For a regular season game. In January. That simply does not happen.

Shaq made some comments before their first matchup that were not exactly respectful, which he later apologized for. What followed was several years of genuinely compelling basketball, two giants trading blows, Yao holding his own, earning respect game by game. By the time their rivalry was in full swing, Shaq had publicly called Yao one of the toughest matchups he faced. From Shaq, that is the basketball equivalent of a standing ovation.

15. The 2018 Season: 65 Wins and the Night That Broke a Million Hearts

The 2017-18 Houston Rockets were special. Not 'pretty good' special. Not 'sneaky playoff team' special. Genuinely, legitimately, best-team-in-the-Western-Conference special. James Harden won MVP. They finished with 65 wins, the best record in the NBA. Their offense was historic. Their three-point shooting was record-setting. Head coach Mike D'Antoni had built something that looked, on paper and in practice, like a genuine championship contender.

They got to Game 7 of the Western Conference Finals against the Golden State Warriors. The Warriors had won three of the previous four championships. This was the moment. Except Houston was already playing shorthanded. Chris Paul had torn his hamstring in Game 5 and never played another minute of the series. He watched Games 6 and 7 from the bench, which is the basketball equivalent of training all year for a marathon and then spraining your ankle the morning of the race.

Houston missed 27 consecutive three-point shots in Game 7. Twenty-seven. In a row. The odds of that happening are roughly the same as being struck by lightning while filling out a winning lottery ticket. The Warriors escaped and went on to win the championship. The Rockets went home. Houston fans sat in their cars for a while, staring at nothing, which is a completely appropriate response. That team deserved better. They just ran out of road at the worst possible time.

Chapter 4: Red Nation, Rockets Culture, and the Weird Stuff

16. Toyota Center and the Loudest Arena in the Southwest

Toyota Center opened in October 2003 and seats just over 18,000 people. On a regular Tuesday in November against a team nobody is scared of, it is a perfectly nice arena. On a playoff night, it transforms into something that feels genuinely dangerous to your eardrums. Visiting players have described walking out for warm-ups and immediately understanding that this was going to be a long evening. The crowd does not ease into it. They arrive loud and get louder, like someone slowly turning up a dial that does not have an off switch.

The court design is legitimately one of the best in the league. Dark background, rocket imagery, Space City branding that actually connects to something real instead of just looking cool on merchandise. When the lights drop before tip-off and the whole building goes dark, there is a moment of complete silence before the Rockets run out and the noise comes back all at once.

Eighteen thousand people going from zero to deafening in about two seconds.

Pretend you are a point guard for the visiting team. You have been in loud arenas before. You think you are ready. Then the lights go out, the countdown starts, and somewhere behind you a section of Red Nation that has been waiting three hours for this exact moment decides it is time. You forget the play you were supposed to run. You forget your own jersey number. You just stand there and accept what is happening to you.

17. Clutch the Bear and the Red Nation Fan Army

The Houston Rockets mascot is a bear. His name is Clutch. The team is called the Rockets, plays in a city built around space exploration, sits twelve miles from NASA's Johnson Space Center, and the character they chose to represent all of that is a bear in a basketball uniform. A bear. Nobody has ever fully explained this decision, and at this point nobody is going to, so we might as well just accept Clutch for who he is and move on with our lives.

What Clutch lacks in thematic consistency he makes up for in sheer chaotic energy. He does dunks off trampolines during timeouts. He fires t-shirts into the upper deck from a cannon. He dances in ways that a bear absolutely should not be able to dance and yet somehow pulls off every single time. He has been doing this since 1995, which means Clutch the Bear has been entertaining Houston fans longer than most of the current roster has been alive. He has at least one championship ring. He is technically a dynasty.

The fan base, Red Nation, is the actual heartbeat of the building. Thousands of people in matching red, loud from the opening tip, the kind of crowd that makes road teams check their calendars twice to make sure they really have to be here tonight. Clutch and Red Nation together are the full package: one bear who defies explanation and eighteen thousand humans who came here specifically to make your life difficult.

18. Space City Swagger: How Houston Shaped the Rockets

Houston is the fourth largest city in the United States and has the energy of a place that does not know or care what number it is. It has more international restaurants per capita than almost anywhere in the country. Its summers are so hot and humid that stepping outside in July feels like walking into the mouth of something large and unhappy. It hosts an actual space program. Its traffic is legendary in ways that cannot be repeated in a children's book. Houston is enormous, loud, diverse, and completely unbothered by your opinion of it.

The Rockets have always been a direct reflection of that personality. This is a franchise that drafted a seven-foot Nigerian center who invented a move nobody could guard, traded for a local hero at the deadline and won a championship with him, brought in the most entertaining thirty-something in basketball just to see what would happen, and in 2018 assembled the best team in the league only to have everything collapse in one of the most specifically cursed ways the sport has ever produced.

The Space City rebrand was not a marketing team inventing an identity from scratch. It was the franchise finally saying out loud what had always been true. You want a team with actual rocket scientists nearby? This is the place. Houston does not give up on launches just because one did not go as planned. It builds a better rocket and tries again.

19. The Harden Beard: A Nickname, a Brand, and an Actual Force of Nature

James Harden's beard is the most famous piece of facial hair in the history of professional basketball, which is a sentence that sounds ridiculous until you realize it is completely and verifiably true. The beard was already impressive when Harden arrived in Houston in 2012. By the time he won MVP in 2018, it had crossed from impressive into something that scientists would probably want to study if they had the time. It did not grow so much as expand. It became structural. It had its own presence in a room.

Sponsors lined up. Harden became one of the most recognizable athletes on the planet not just because he was an extraordinary basketball player, which he absolutely was, but because the beard preceded him everywhere he went like an announcement. There are commercials where the beard enters the frame before Harden does. Children who had never watched an NBA game recognized the beard the way they recognized cartoon characters.

What gets lost in the beard mythology is that Harden needed zero help being famous. Nine All-Star appearances. Five scoring titles. One MVP. A 36-point-per-game scoring average across a full season, the highest since Michael Jordan in 1987. The beard was extraordinary. The player attached to it was on another level entirely. Though if the beard ever filed for independent recognition, the Hall of Fame committee would at minimum have to hold a meeting about it.

20. Yao's Impact Off the Court: How One Player Changed Global Basketball

Before Yao Ming showed up in Houston in 2002, the NBA had some fans in China. After Yao Ming showed up, the NBA had China. That is the entire difference, stated as plainly as possible, and it is not a small one.

Games featuring Yao were broadcast to audiences in China that dwarfed anything the NBA had previously achieved internationally. Regular season games in

November, games that American fans might half-watch while doing something else, were drawing tens of millions of Chinese viewers who set alarms, stayed up through the night, and organized their entire week around tip-off time. Houston Rockets jerseys became some of the best-selling pieces of sports merchandise on earth. The NBA opened offices in China. Revenue from the Chinese market grew into a number with a lot of zeros.

He retired in 2011, became president of the Chinese Basketball Association, got elected to the Naismith Memorial Basketball Hall of Fame, and in doing all of this managed to be impressive in about four different careers before most people have figured out one. Yao Ming arrived in Houston as a basketball player and left as the reason an entire generation of kids on the other side of the planet grew up with a favorite NBA team. The least Houston could do was retire his number, which they did, immediately, without hesitation, because some things are just obvious.

Chapter 5: The Next Launch: Houston's Future

21. The Rebuild Begins: How Houston Turned Losses Into Lottery Picks

Between 2021 and 2023, the Houston Rockets were not good at basketball. They were historically, magnificently, almost artistically not good at basketball. They lost 20 games in a row at one point. They finished with the worst record in the entire NBA two seasons running. Going to a Rockets game during this period was less of a sporting event and more of a philosophical experience. You sat there. You watched. You questioned things.

But here is the secret the Rockets front office knew that casual fans did not: losing on purpose is actually a strategy. A real one. The NBA gives the worst teams the best chances at the top picks in the draft, which means if you are going to be terrible, you should at least be terrible with a plan. Houston collected draft picks the way your uncle collects things he sees at car boot sales, except instead of broken lamps and weird china, Houston was collecting future NBA players. Their own picks. Other teams' picks. Picks so far in the future that analysts needed a calendar from a different decade to track them all.

Every great modern dynasty went through this exact process first. The San Antonio Spurs lost deliberately to get Tim Duncan. The Golden State Warriors bottomed out before Steph Curry arrived. Oklahoma City rebuilt quietly and then showed up one day with Kevin Durant. Houston watched all of them, took notes, and waited. The picks arrived. The players developed. The losses stopped. The countdown is very much underway.

22. Alperen Sengun: The Turkish Treasure Running the Paint

Alperen Sengun was born in Sakarya, Turkey, grew up playing basketball there, and arrived in Houston at nineteen years old looking like someone who had already figured out a large portion of the game that other players spend their entire careers trying to understand. He plays center. He is listed at six feet nine inches. He has the footwork of a point guard, the passing instincts of someone who can see two seconds into the future, and a post game so developed that NBA scouts watched his film and then watched it again because they assumed they had missed something.

What makes Sengun genuinely special is that he does things in the post that centers twice his age do not do. He catches the ball with his back to the basket, reads the defense in about half a second, and then either scores, passes to an open teammate, or draws a foul. Opposing coaches have described preparing a game plan for him and then watching him do something completely different from what they prepared for anyway. He is like showing up to argue with someone and discovering they already know every point you were planning to make.

He earned his first All-Star selection in 2026, a sign that the rest of the league is starting to catch up to what Houston already knew. Sengun does not celebrate like he just discovered fire. He nods, gets back on defense, and does it again. Houston found a genuinely special player, and the terrifying part is he is still only in his early twenties.

23. Jalen Green: Highlight Reel on Legs

Jalen Green was selected second overall in the 2021 draft, one spot behind Cade Cunningham, which is a fact that will be argued about on basketball Twitter until the sun burns out. Houston took him without hesitation, and the reason is simple: Jalen Green can do things with a basketball that make the people watching them happen audibly gasp, then look at the person next to them, then look back at the court, then shake their heads slowly like they are trying to clear water from their ears.

He is 6 feet 4 inches, built like someone designed him specifically to be impossible to contain off the dribble, and has a first step that is genuinely offensive. As in, it should be illegal. Defenders who prepare for it, who watch film of it, who know exactly when it is coming, still get left standing in place looking like a traffic cone that somebody drove past at full speed. He averaged over 22 points per game in the 2024-25 season and is still, at 23 years old, clearly figuring out how good he is going to be, which is a deeply unfair situation for every other team in the Western Conference.

Pairing Sengun and Green together is Houston's big bet. One player who processes the game like a chess grandmaster, one player who treats defenders like minor inconveniences on his way to the basket. They are young enough that their best basketball is still ahead of them, which should make Red Nation extremely excited and everyone else extremely nervous.

24. Ime Udoka: The Coach Who's Seen It All

Ime Udoka has had a career path that would take a very long time to fully explain at a dinner party. He played in the NBA for seven seasons, mostly as a defensive specialist and role player, never a star but always the kind of guy that teams wanted in the locker room because he made everything around him more serious. He went into coaching, worked his way up through several staffs, and in 2021 became head coach of the Boston Celtics, where he immediately took them to the NBA Finals in his very first season as a head coach. First season. Finals.

Then some complicated off-court situations happened, he ended up leaving Boston, and Houston hired him in 2023 to coach the young Rockets. The Celtics, for the record, went on to win the championship two years later with the team Udoka had largely built. This is the kind of thing that would cause a normal person to need a very long walk and possibly several conversations with a therapist. Udoka showed up in Houston, looked at his young roster, and got to work.

What Udoka brings to a rebuilding team is exactly what a rebuilding team needs: someone who has been in a Finals, who knows what that pressure feels like, who can look a 21-year-old in the eyes and say with complete credibility that this is what it takes. For a team full of players who have never been anywhere near a championship, having a coach who can describe exactly what the path looks and feels like is worth more than any motivational poster anyone has ever put on a locker room wall.

25. Why Houston's Next Chapter Might Be the Most Exciting Yet

Here is where everything lands. Sengun at center. Green on the wing. A pile of draft picks that have not been used yet. A coach who has stood in the Finals and knows the way back. An arena full of Red Nation fans who watched two years of painful rebuilding without turning the lights off. And a city that has already won two NBA championships and has absolutely no intention of treating that history as a ceiling.

The Western Conference is brutal. It always is. The Oklahoma City Thunder are young and terrifying. The Golden State Warriors have been doing this longer than some of Houston's players have been alive. The Denver Nuggets, the Memphis Grizzlies, the Minnesota Timberwolves, all of them dangerous, all of them hungry. Getting through the West to a championship is like trying to win a footrace where half the other runners have secretly been training in the mountains for three years without telling anyone.

But here is the thing about Houston. This franchise turned a man who had never played basketball at seventeen into the greatest center of a generation. It traded for a hometown hero at the deadline and won a title. It drafted a Turkish teenager and an electric California kid and decided those two were going to be the core of the next great era. It has Clutch the Bear, who has two rings and zero explanations for his own existence. The Rockets have been building something real. The fuse is lit. Space City does not do quiet launches.

Bonus Trivia Quiz!

You think you are a true Houston Rockets fan? Try this bonus quiz!

1. Where did the Houston Rockets play before moving to Houston?

A) Portland, Oregon
B) San Diego, California
C) Seattle, Washington
D) Phoenix, Arizona

2. What is the name of NASA's facility located near Houston that became the city's most famous landmark?

A) Kennedy Space Center
B) Cape Canaveral
C) Johnson Space Center
D) Jet Propulsion Laboratory

3. Moses Malone was famous for doing what better than almost anyone who ever played the game?

A) Shooting three-pointers
B) Stealing passes
C) Rebounding
D) Drawing fouls

4. What nickname did Houston earn after coming back from two separate 3-1 series deficits in the 1995 playoffs?

A) Space City
B) Comeback City
C) Clutch City
D) Rocket City

5. What was the name of the unstoppable post move that Hakeem Olajuwon invented and used to torture every center who ever tried to guard him?

A) The Sky Hook
B) The Dream Shake
C) The Nigerian Spin
D) The Houston Shuffle

6. Clyde Drexler grew up in Houston, went to college in Houston, and then spent most of his career playing for which team before finally coming home?

A) The Seattle SuperSonics
B) The Phoenix Suns
C) The Portland Trail Blazers
D) The Denver Nuggets

7. Charles Barkley, Hakeem Olajuwon, and Clyde Drexler playing together were nicknamed what by fans?

A) The Big Three

B) The Three Kings

C) The Dream Team

D) The Space Cowboys

8. How tall was Yao Ming?

A) 7 feet 1 inch

B) 7 feet 3 inches

C) 7 feet 5 inches

D) 7 feet 6 inches

9. James Harden won the NBA MVP award in which season?

A) 2015-16

B) 2016-17

C) 2017-18

D) 2018-19

10. In the 1994 NBA Finals, Houston beat which team to win the franchise's first championship?

A) The New York Knicks

B) The Chicago Bulls

C) The Orlando Magic

D) The Utah Jazz

11. During the 2018 Western Conference Finals against the Golden State Warriors, what happened to Chris Paul in Game 5 that changed everything?

A) He fouled out in the third quarter
B) He injured his hamstring and could not return
C) He was ejected for arguing with a referee
D) He missed 15 consecutive free throws

12. What is the name of the Houston Rockets mascot, and what animal is he?

A) Blaze, a lion
B) Turbo, a cheetah
C) Clutch, a bear
D) Rocket, a dog

13. Before Hakeem Olajuwon ever picked up a basketball, what sport did he play growing up in Nigeria?

A) Cricket and track
B) Handball and soccer
C) Rugby and swimming
D) Tennis and volleyball

14. Alperen Sengun, Houston's young star center, was born in which country?

A) Serbia

B) Greece

C) Turkey

D) Croatia

15. How many consecutive three-point shots did the Rockets miss during Game 7 of the 2018 Western Conference Finals against the Warriors?

A) 14

B) 19

C) 23

D) 27

Super Fan Secret Challenge

Only a true Houston Rockets fan will know this.

(No Answer Provided)

In what round of the 1994 NBA Playoffs did Houston eliminate the Phoenix Suns on their way to the championship, and who led the Rockets in scoring in that series?

A) Second Round; Hakeem Olajuwon
B) Conference Finals; Clyde Drexler
C) First Round; Vernon Maxwell
D) Conference Semifinals; Kenny Smith

Answer Key

1. B) San Diego, California

2. C) Johnson Space Center

3. C) Rebounding

4. C) Clutch City

5. B) The Dream Shake

6. C) The Portland Trail Blazers

7. B) The Three Kings

8. D) 7 feet 6 inches

9. C) 2017-18

10. A) The New York Knicks

11. B) He injured his hamstring and could not return

12. C) Clutch, a bear

13. B) Handball and soccer

14. C) Turkey

15. D) 27

NBA PLAYOFF BRACKET

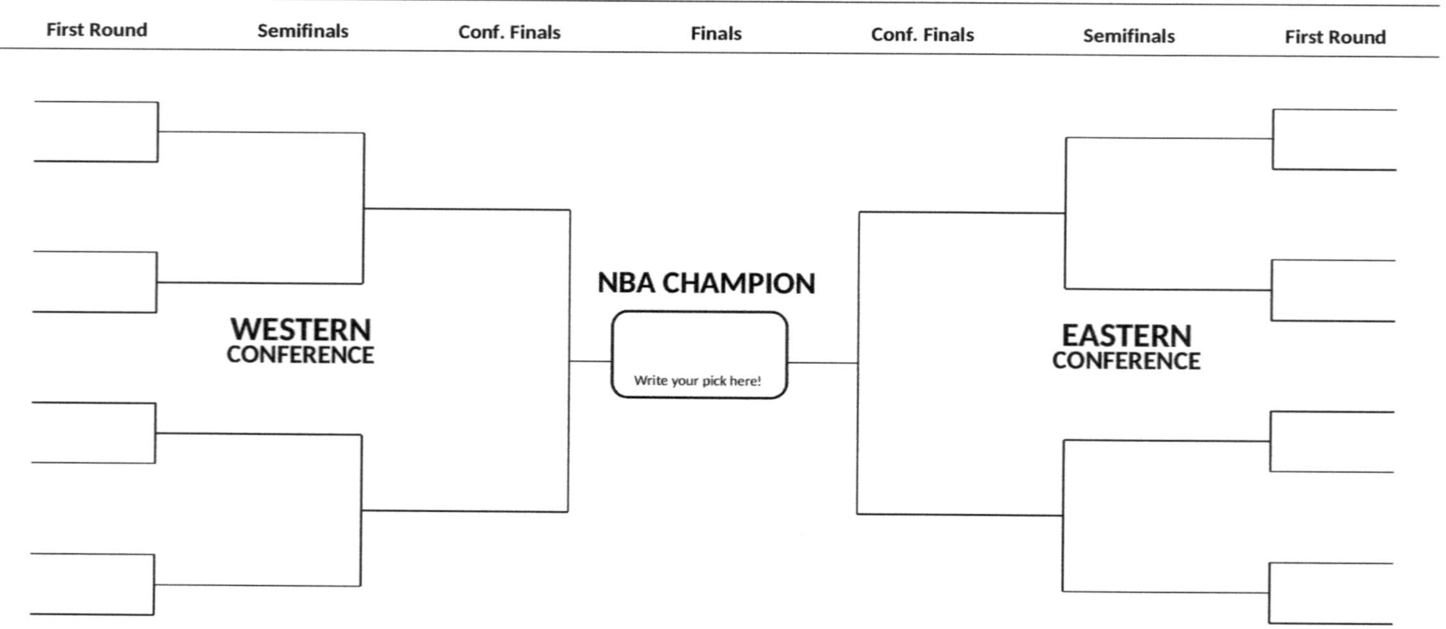

* Fill in your picks and try not to argue with your friends about it!

Part of the Fun Fan Facts: The Unofficial Sports Guide Series

Be the Boss of the Playoffs

You've broken down the matchups. You know which superstar takes over in the fourth quarter. You've seen the bench units that quietly decide series. You've watched the adjustments coaches make when their backs are against the wall.

Now it's time to stop watching and start deciding.

On this page, you are not just a fan. You are the Head Coach drawing up the last play with three seconds left on the clock. You are the GM who built this roster. You are the analyst who saw it all coming.

This is not just filling out a bracket.

This is building your championship run.

Sixteen teams enter the NBA Playoffs. The path is brutal. Best of seven. No shortcuts. No hiding. Every round gets louder, harder, and more personal.

This bracket is your Playoff Control Room.

The Game Plan

1. Survive Round One: Start with the opening round. Which matchup is going seven games? Who has the closer? Who folds under pressure? Make the calls.

2. Feel the Momentum: As you move into the Conference Semifinals and Conference Finals, things change. Role players become heroes. Stars feel the weight. Trust your reads.

3. Own the Finals: Trace your picks all the way to the NBA Finals. When the confetti falls and the trophy is raised, you'll find out who earned it.

House Rules: Circle your boldest upset. That is your official "I knew it" moment.

Choose Your Weapon: Pencil if you want flexibility. Pen if you trust your instincts. Sharpie if you believe in chaos.

Because once the playoffs tip off, there is no rewinding Game 7.

Make your picks. Trust your basketball brain. And let the playoff drama begin.

Fun Facts Wrap-Up

You made it through! You're officially a true superfan! Now it's time to put your knowledge to the test. Share these facts with friends and see who really knows their team best.

Love the series?

Your reviews help other fans discover Fun Fan Facts. If you enjoyed this book, we'd really appreciate you sharing your thoughts and leaving a review.

Want more Fun Fan Facts?

Scan the QR code below to visit our site and explore bonus trivia, challenges, and special extras - including new teams, future series, and collectible fun as they're released.

Collect All the Fun Fan Facts Series!

Check off every book you read. See the full set on Amazon. Search "Fun Fan Facts Jake Liam."

World Cup 2026 Edition

☐ Algeria

☐ Argentina

☐ Australia

☐ Austria

☐ Belgium

☐ Brazil

☐ Canada

☐ Cape Verde

☐ Colombia

☐ Croatia

☐ Curaçao

☐ Ecuador

☐ Egypt

☐ England

☐ France

☐ Germany

☐ Ghana

☐ Haiti

☐ Iran

☐ Ivory Coast

☐ Japan

☐ Jordan

☐ Mexico

☐ Morocco

☐ Netherlands

☐ New Zealand

☐ Norway

☐ Panama

☐ Paraguay

☐ Portugal

☐ Qatar

☐ Saudi Arabia

☐ Scotland

☐ Senegal

☐ South Africa

☐ South Korea

☐ Spain

☐ Switzerland

☐ Tunisia

☐ United States

☐ Uruguay

☐ Uzbekistan

World Cup 2026 Group Edition

☐ Group A

☐ Group B

☐ Group C

☐ Group D

☐ Group E

☐ Group F

☐ Group G

☐ Group H

☐ Group I

☐ Group J

☐ Group K

☐ Group L

English Football Edition

☐ Arsenal F.C. ☐ Manchester City

☐ Aston Villa F.C. ☐ Manchester United

☐ Chelsea F.C. ☐ Newcastle United F.C.

☐ Everton F.C. ☐ Tottenham Hotspur

☐ Fulham F.C. ☐ West Ham United

☐ Liverpool F.C. ☐ Wrexham A.F.C.

NBA Edition

☐ Atlanta Hawks ☐ Miami Heat

☐ Boston Celtics ☐ Milwaukee Bucks

☐ Brooklyn Nets ☐ Minnesota Timberwolves

☐ Charlotte Hornets ☐ New Orleans Pelicans

☐ Chicago Bulls ☐ New York Knicks

☐ Cleveland Cavaliers ☐ Oklahoma City Thunder

☐ Dallas Mavericks ☐ Orlando Magic

☐ Denver Nuggets ☐ Philadelphia 76ers

☐ Detroit Pistons ☐ Phoenix Suns

☐ Golden State Warriors ☐ Portland Trail Blazers

☐ Houston Rockets ☐ Sacramento Kings

☐ Indiana Pacers ☐ San Antonio Spurs

☐ LA Clippers ☐ Toronto Raptors

☐ Los Angeles Lakers ☐ Utah Jazz

☐ Memphis Grizzlies ☐ Washington Wizards

About the Author

Jake is a 13-year-old sports fan who loves football, American football, and basketball. He plays soccer as a goalie and dreams of one day playing for West Ham United and helping teach kids to love the game. His passion for sports runs in the family - his dad was a professional baseball player, and his stepdad sparked his love for West Ham. Through the Fun Fan Facts series, he shares the fun and excitement of sports with fans everywhere.